T0150782

TIGER GIRL

Pascale Petit was born in Paris, grew up in France and Wales and lives in Cornwall. She is of French/Welsh/Indian heritage. Her eighth collection, *Tiger Girl* (Bloodaxe Books, 2020), is shortlisted for the 2020 Forward Prize for Best Collection, and a poem from the book won the 2020 Keats-Shelley Poetry Prize. Her previous collection, *Mama Amazonica* (Bloodaxe Books, 2017), won the RSL Ondaatje Prize 2018, was a Poetry Book Society Choice, was shortlisted for the Roehampton Poetry Prize 2018, and is longlisted for the inaugural Laurel Prize. She published six earlier collections, four of which were shortlisted for the T.S. Eliot Prize, most recently, her sixth collection, *Fauverie* (Seren, 2014). A portfolio of poems from that book won the 2013 Manchester Poetry Prize.

Her fifth collection, *What the Water Gave Me: Poems after Frida Kahlo*, published by Seren in 2010 (UK) and Black Lawrence Press in 2011 (US), was shortlisted for both the T.S. Eliot Prize and Wales Book of the Year.

She received a Cholmondeley Award from the Society of Authors in 2015, and was the chair of the judges for the 2015 T.S. Eliot Prize. Her books have been translated into Spanish, Chinese, Serbian and French. She is widely travelled in the Peruvian and Venezuelan Amazon, as well as in China, Kazakhstan, Nepal, Mexico and India. Trained as a sculptor at the Royal College of Art, she spent the first part of her life as a visual artist.

PASCALE PETIT

Tiger Girl

BLOODAXE BOOKS

ISBN: 978 1 78037 526 7

First published 2020 by
Bloodaxe Books Ltd,
Eastburn,
South Park,
Hexham,
Northumberland NE46 1BS.

www.bloodaxebooks.com
For further information about Bloodaxe titles
please visit our website and join our mailing list
or write to the above address for a catalogue.

Supported using public funding by
ARTS COUNCIL
ENGLAND

Cover design: Neil Astley & Pamela Robertson-Pearce.

Printed in Great Britain by Bell & Bain Limited, Glasgow, Scotland, on
acid-free paper sourced from mills with FSC chain of custody certification.

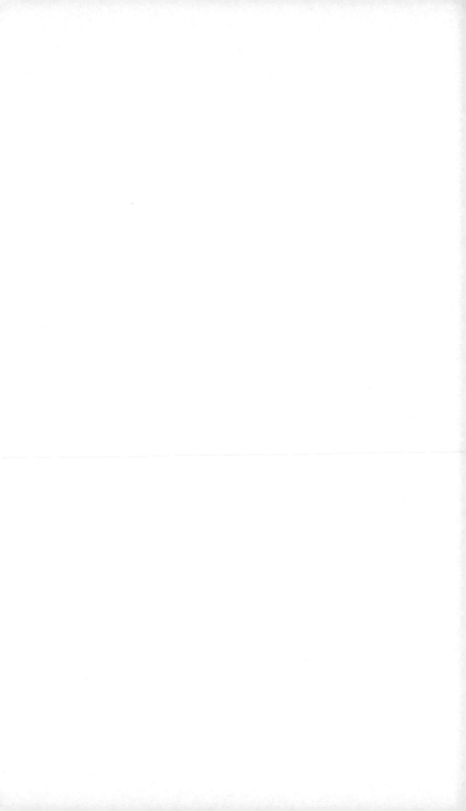

CONTENTS

Her Gypsy Clothes

I used to wonder why my grandmother
stared so hard into the fire
                    even after I found the cardboard box
at the back of the coal-house
                    and drew out of it

flame   chilli   emerald
sequin sparks
        embroidered mirrors
                orbiting wraparound skirts

shawls trimmed with seedpearls
silver bangles like Saturn's rings

Her embarrassment when she caught me trying them on
and explained they were her gypsy rags
                to tell fortunes at fairs

Only at her funeral did the story come out –
        her birth in Rajasthan to her father's maid

I think now of my great-grandmother dancing
for her master's guests   grateful
to have her baby   brought up as his wife's

I think of the coal grease   black dust
and memories that burn   slow as anthracite

        how some colours don't fade
                however deep they're buried

                    how even a dowry of rags
smouldering in a box
                    can flare in a winter grate

and how   to own the country of her birth
                    a woman might have to wear   a fire

The Umbrella Stand

What I remember is running my hands along the hide,
how wrinkled it was, how hard the polished nails,
each big as my hand. How I used to hide inside,
until one day Daddy said I'd been crouching
in the forefoot of an elephant he hunted tigers on.
How an angry tigress had leapt onto his mount
and bit into her spine. How, even after death,
the matriarch was useful. How long it took to scoop out
the flesh, rub the interior with arsenic soap, soften
the skin by soaking in warm water, then to dry it in the sun,
packed with sand, coir forced into each toe.

I still play hide and seek in her, and once, curled up,
fell asleep, rocked by the sway of a stately walk.
I felt every stone and flattened bush, a trunk
lowered to caress me, the branches of Indian beech
brushing my head. And high up in the sky,
my father riding on a pad of cloud –
my hero, who killed the man-eater.
I was woken by his face peering down where
once there was a knee, him saying how much
he loved me, but how I'd have to fend for myself
when he goes, to beware of his wife, my second mother.

It was then he told me the family secret – that
our hill-tribe maid was really my mam.
Sometimes I see the tigress hanging by her claws,
the explosion of her face, the black and tan lightning
that bursts from her muzzle, and the sky collapses –
all twenty tons of monsoon grey, all the rain
that's fallen in my life since Daddy died.
I wake in the umbrella stand. Only, there is no

rain left, just the sun drying me out, my flesh
scooped up, sand poured in my body, arsenic
rubbed inside, my skin varnished and coated with lampblack.

In the Forest

In the forest I saw a man
sewing an owl's eyes shut

the owl was on a leash
and the man pulled it to make it flutter
and attract songbirds to mob his decoy.

He told me how much he could earn
from warblers in cages.

I wondered which was worse –
the blind eagle owl
or thrushes glued to sticks.

The deeper I went the more I saw.

What is worse asked the sky –
a girl with sewn eyes or glued lips?

The deeper I walked the harder I looked
although it was dark
and there were no stars.

4,000 rupees for a barn owl
to be sacrificed for Diwali

to light up the dark
with dark.

I went even deeper into the core
patrolled by forest guards on tuskers
but it was night and the bulls were chained.

I saw another man who led me to a cave
which he called his vault
and there was a tigress inside
giving birth to striped gold.

I said my eyes are stitched
and my lips sealed
and he placed coins in my hand
said it was jungle currency

and I knew then I was holding
the eyes of cubs.

I said to the poacher I'm not from here
I do not judge

but the eyes mewled in my hands

so I ran through every coppice
and every clearing
and looked at the moon
whose eye was sewn shut.

I passed the firefly tree
and the flame-of-the-forest
and I swear there were leopards
dangling from their boughs.

I came to the crocodile bark tree
and the ghost tree
as the first rays peered through night's lids

but the sun couldn't look at what I had seen

the sun couldn't wake the sambar,
chital, antelope or gazelle.

So I was the only witness
of those luminous herds
with fire trees on the altars of their brows –

all sacrificed for good fortune.

Goddess Lakshmi forgive them
as you ride your owls.

And that was long ago now
but still I'm running through that forest

watched by the moon-eye
and the sun-eye –

~

But now it's a forest of peeling red bark
of leopards with paws sawn off
stuffed into pockets
for luck

while in the tantrik market
a trader slices a tiger
giving it new stripes –
one stripe for a lakh of rupees.

I run through thickets of dust trees
until I reach the realm of the sloth bear
where a cub clings
to his electrocuted mother

and here I find a man laughing
as he hooks a cane
through the cub's nose
and teaches him to dance.

The night is black as bear fur

its muzzle bleeding after eating honey
baited with explosives.

How many rupees for the galaxies
in a gall bladder?

~

I run more slowly now, afraid
of traps for my ankles, snares for my neck.

You could say my flight is a jerky dance
the stars my audience with shielded eyes

because the ringmaster has arrived in heaven
with his flaming hoops
archangels must leap through.

Where are the angels with fangs that sever windpipes?
Angel-fangs around a black hole's neck
bought in the black market.

Goddess Durga who rides the sky-tiger
forgive us.

You could say
the stick that makes my head jerk
is a bad branch from the tree of life

but I swear there's a tree of good
if only I could find it
for the cub that survived

whose claws are new moons
that light up my path

and even though it's day now
the forest has drawn blinds over itself.

~

I climb a hide and as I climb
the trees grow higher.
Banyan boles pierce the ladder
and hiss like snakes with skeleton leaves.

I pass choirs of langurs
with silver fur and ebony faces
their echoing barks getting louder.

But even up here vendors are shouting
ten crore for a white tiger
five crore for a black leopard.

Here where the blacksmith forges
leg traps in the night market.

Here too there are trees with scratch marks
but no tigers

unless you count the meat without skin
all bones pulled out –
for just one rib of baagh can buy a cow.

Let me tell you what I saw
let me whisper it.

I saw an archangel with its paw
mangled in a trap for what seemed
an aeon

I saw a man waiting for it to weaken
while he ate his meal on a teak leaf.
And when he had finished
I saw him whittle a stick

and when the archangel
was too weak to move
he jabbed his stick into its mouth

so no one would hear its music.

I saw him pick up a branch
and batter the spine

and I knew then that the branch
was from the tree of secrets
for how else did he know
where creatures of light walk on our earth

their footprints that glow on the path
saying *This way This way to my kingdom.*

Then the man got out his skinning knife.
Half an hour it took him
to flay the hide intact

with its arabesques of bulldozed gardens.

If it were possible to remake the creature
from its pelt I would do it

but the man sold the pelt
because his family was hungry.

And I vowed then never to eat again.

I descended the spiral ladder
and with bamboo thorns and plant fibre
I sewed my eyes shut

and with resin from the tree of love
I glued my lips.

Green Bee-eater

More precious than all
the gems of Jaipur –

the green bee-eater.

If you see one singing
tree-tree-tree

with his space-black bill
and rufous cap,

his robes
all shades of emerald

like treetops glimpsed
from a plane,

his blue cheeks,
black eye-mask

and the delicate tail streamer
like a plume of smoke –

you might dream
of the forests

that once clothed
our flying planet.

And perhaps his singing
is a spell

to call our forests back –

tree
    by *tree*
        by *tree.*

Surprised!

When lightning flickers over my cot
and the air tingles

with the electric charge
of the great cat's fur –

      I cross into the night
      where my jungle tent is pitched.

I am a child staring
into green flames,

wondering who is this angel
crouched above me,

      her coat of icicles,
      her eyes like meteors
      shooting into my face.

My hand is a brave monkey
reaching up to touch her fangs –

      while all the hairs of my body
      rise like wind in a storm

      as she brands me with her stripes.

My Mugger Crib

My crib is made of tanned crocodile skin.
I lie inside her as she belly-walks
along the riverbed of my sleep.

Mother whispers bedtime stories –
what my crib eats, the deer she drags underwater
to soften before pulling off limbs.

Mother leaves me in the jungle tent alone
and says I'll be safe because my crib
will mug any tiger that comes near.

I stay submerged, only my eyes and snout
above the quilt, while my magar
tells me how she got here, the men

who stood on her head and tail,
while another slit the skin of her neck
and pushed a rod down her spine

to loosen the hide. How she lay there
for days without her armour,
until death eased the pain.

When the tigress comes into my tent,
her teats swinging, newly milked,
she sees a baby covered in scales,

a cattle egret riding on her
like the guardian of infancy.
She senses the mugger in her laying trance,

the mammy who once carried hatchlings
in her throat-pouch to the nursery pools.
These are my true mothers: a marsh titan

who hears my ultrasonic cries, a nursing tigress –
all the animals who came that night
to watch over me, who watch over me still.

Her Tigress Eyes

When I met you that first evening
and I was a seven-year-old perched
on your settee, not understanding English,
all I could see was your eyes. I also sensed
the queen of India in a double exposure,
the summer sky reflected in her irises,
sapphire glints from her father, Blue Eyes,
among golden groves of rods and cones.
Behind the tigress, your black eyes
glistened with forest ferns, birds
nested between them, your glasses
made your living room a fairy green.
Did I dream awake? Or was I hallucinating
after the night crossing and long drive to Wales,
or the surprise of being left in a place
where I could start to sprout roots.
Perhaps I recalled being here before
as a baby – because however unfamiliar
it felt, with the strange language, the animals
that surrounded us as if I'd landed in paradise –
I knew I was back home. Your eyes
told me this when you looked at me,
your hands making the sign for food and milk,
just as a tigress attends to her cub, licks her
of dangerous scents, and brings her
spirit-deer from the meadow. Then, over
the years, through example, goes on
to teach her how to hunt for herself,
how to survive among the teeth and claws
she will have to one day battle.
Seven years I thrived in your warmth,
and at the end, you batted me away
to go find my own territory, my own strength.

Tiger Gran

My grandmother of the flying electric blanket,
who speaks Hindi in her sleep,
who has gharials in her black eyes
behind steamed-up glasses, a long nose
like a mountain between two countries – one hot, one cold.
Who mothered me when I was newborn,
and saved me from going to the bad.

My grandmother who returned me to my mother twice,
which meant orphanage, which meant other people's homes.
My grandmother who took me back
for seven years from age seven, who saved my life,
praise to the mothering of my tigress!
My grandmother who works at the chippie, who takes in
neighbours' washing, who cleans big houses,

who makes me work in the garden for my keep,
for whom I would weed the world,
for whom I would pump the Severn to save her black hybrids,
for she is a hybrid rose who has been saved.
My grandmother who keeps a jungle folded in her greenhouse,
who lets me join her in its heat-heart.
My grandmother whom I catch peeing among the plant pots,

who explains she has only one kidney
and can't always make it to our toilet.
My grandmother whose hair fell out
when they removed her kidney without anaesthetic
while she was pregnant with my uncle.
My grandmother who shouts *Avert your eyes!* when she undresses,
so I won't see the permanent tan under her clothes.

My grandmother with the curse of second sight
but the blessing of second birth to her father's wife
so her real mother, the maid, would not be stoned.
My grandmother who was left alone in a jungle tent
by her white step-mother, for the tiger to eat,
who, when we are riding the winged blanket,
tells me how she watched the vision enter

and reached out to touch its dazzle, who was spared
because she was not afraid, who held
the wonder's gaze and saw its icicle teeth drip
on the red tongue at the gate of paradise
but did not go down that carpet into the tunnel.
My tawny grandma with as many wrinkles as tributaries
in the Ganges, her face the map of India when it's summer,

the map of Wales in winter. And sometimes her wrinkles
are stripes that scare me if I look at her
when she is flying the tails of her stories.
She who was left to run wild by her doting father
when she wasn't slaving for his white family,
who I am allowed to cuddle so I can sleep.
My grandmother the tiger-girl. The Untouchable.

Indian Roller

Once when I was in your double bed
and it wasn't dark yet, twilight
through the bare windows either side of us,

I asked you the name of the deep blue
the sky was turning, and you said *neelkanth,*
some daylight still on its wings,

but only when airborne
do we see the colour heaven must be,
night and day dancing a duo

when the roller wheels and soars.
Now that I'm the age you were then,
I can tell you how we are hurtling

towards the Great Attractor veiled behind
the Milky Way in the Zone of Avoidance,
that we are flying even while lying down.

I can look back and see the blue plumes
that jet from your skin, my grandmother,
while you journey in your mind towards India

under our aqua-quilt, ultramarine sheets,
solar wind for pillows, and I want
to keep us in that make-believe heat.

I'm not going to tell you what happens
next, that in Hyderabad where you once lived,
there grew a market called Murgi Chowk –

a bazaar of cages, of tied feet, glued wings.
I'm not going to break your heart by saying
when you sent me back to my mother

she glued my wings together to stop me escaping.
Let's visit that childhood haunt together,
let's buy a blue captive to release.

Let's release all the rollers for our sins
to be forgiven, let's not know how
the bird charmers recapture them – to sell again.

Her Bulbul

She calls me her little bulbul
because I've nested in her house,
and she brushes my hair
when I sing at her feet.

She too sings of a time
when her mother called her bulbul,
brushing a hundred strokes
while monkeys played in her coils.

Her mother the maid, looking after children
wild as tiger cubs,
in groves ringed by electric wires
to protect them from hunters.

See how our hair sparks
and our feathers growl
under poachers' hands.
Our heads covered in dust

of dried-up riverbeds.
My grandmother sang and sings still,
teaching me the words
in the old language,

of how a wood can grow from a twig,
how each note is an egg
balanced on barbed wire,
and in each egg an unbroken world.

When I was eight my father visited and we went fishing

After my father came in while I was sleeping
and lay on top of me as if I was nothing
but a riverbed he needed to flow over –
        I dreamt of fish with children's faces,

then I stopped sleeping.
Even now, I can only drift off
if I picture myself sinking into deep water.
        I open my lips and let the tongue

of blackwater tasting of sewage
slide in, against the back of my throat,
to flood my stomach with ice, my face
        silver-green as that day's catch,

how he slapped the perch against his knee,
her mouth wide open, gasping,
her face a mirror of scales –
        her eyes still glare at me as I gut her.

Mongoose Brushes

After my father left, my grandmother called me
her little mongoose – her Rikki-Tikki-Tavi –
clever enough to kill the cobra under her bed,
which is where I hid when I was frightened.

Long after Father left, I learnt how men trap
mongooses in nets, then beat them with clubs,
how sometimes they even flay them
before they are dead, to sell their fur to dealers.

So, when I decided to become a painter,
and longed for the finest brushes, I prayed
that none of them were mongoose hair.
I prayed that even the precocious teenager

I would become, desperate to be pretty,
wouldn't need such soft make-up brushes.
I wanted to ban the newspapers my father
read at the table, the black and white telly

that showed us the cruel world.
My grandmother kept saying my father
was charming, the perfect gentleman,
but I want him to stop arriving

as he's been doing all my life, bringing
his tales of small mammals and what's
done to them, while he skins me
with one glance down my eight-year-old body.

Chital Girl

1

Look at that chital draped on the tree –

a leopard dragged her up
        just as the doe was giving birth to me.

That tree whose leaves are eyes
trying to close
             as he lifts
his bloody nose from her pelvis.

2

Scratch the bark and you'll fall
into interstellar space.

        Night is a brown scab
        my dreams scrape   as if

I could reach the antlered star forest.

3

Look down at the tigress
who stood between me and the leopard,

who fought him off
             then nursed me on her milk.

How long will she mistake me for her cub?

4

Night drips my mother's blood
        onto my face.

        Night is a birth-cord the leopard tugs.

        Dawn is when it rips.

Dawn is a spiny tongue
licking afterbirth from my eyes.

5

Look at my markings – are these
the white spots of a deer

or the black spots of the beast?

I don't know who I am. Perhaps
I should be striped like the other cubs
        in this village.

I don't know when my guardian
will chase me from her den

and send me back to the ghost tree.

Pump

I've just had the needle and my arm's still
sore, but there are ten tin tubs to fill,
not for washing – though I step over
mounds of neighbours' smelly socks –
but for your roses in the drought.
I'm counting to a hundred as water spurts.

Fifty years later I'm in an Indian jungle,
the Gypsy parked at a waterhole
and look who's lounging on the far shore
setting off bursts of paparazzi fire –
the subadult male, his markings
ripples of a shirred pool at dawn.

My arm aches from trying to hold
the zoom steady, his face a blurred
golden double bloom that comes into focus
and I'm still pumping, still young,
and you're fussing with tubs, carrying
lifelines out to your Rosa mundis

with their sunrise and sunset streaks.
And soon I'll crouch among the tangles
of claws and petal faces, the fur-
black soil, drawing the creatures that
crawled up the long green tunnels
to open their ravenous jaws.

Never again will I look so hard, or see
how savage your roses could grow,
their facial disks that roared
all that summer, as my crayons
poured lifeblood onto the paper while
the valves of my heart worked their pump.

Her Globe

This amber-emerald globe, its metamorphic
lustre, the chrysoprase of its
chatoyant forests, crystal thickets
echoing with alarm calls, streaked with
ultraviolet urine, territorial scat, hotspots
where a chital's hooves have sparked.
Every time she tells the future is a ride
into the convex mirror of a tiger's eye
glowing in the tented dark, her customer
just a flicker on the sea's horizon.
Your grandmother was a witch, my mother says,
deep and sly. I evade her grasp
by sliding into the scrying ball's fire.
Cicadas shrill in the branch tunnel
above me and the hawk-cuckoo drills
his brainfever chant – a rising scream
auguring rain, monsoon season
when Central India's national parks close
and the jeep tracks flood quicksilver.
Tigers lounge in flash-pools with their cubs.
Bhitri the ravine tigress abandons her cave
to splash in the shallows. Shy Bhitri,
meaning 'the deep place', screened fissure
where unnamed trees thrust through glass groves
of torrential showers towards the light.
Even her mother Banbehi is flushed out,
descendant of Sita, pride of Bandhavgarh,
the first to survive long enough to found
a dynasty before the poachers got to her.
My grandmother sits in the fair's fortune-
telling booth, decked in her gypsy veils.
They whirl around her like cumulus clouds

at sunset. I hunch in the corner while flame-
backed woodpeckers flash past to drum
on lightning trees. The last ribbon of altocirrus
is a paradise flycatcher's tail streamers.
The crystal ball pulses in Gran's hands.
Her face floats on the surface then is sucked in,
as if our earth has inner globes
nested inside, whirlpools of spiralling
planets opening their diamond mines,
and she, the only adventurer to brave their deeps.
Your Gran was a witch, Mother repeats,
and you take after her. I stare into space until
the globe appears, can feel it heavy on my lap.
Soon, I'm back in the forest maze
where Gran is my guide. With all her power
I pass into the future, leaving only a trace of myself
like dust on the surface of a mirror.

Her Mouth

When they accuse her of being a witch
my grandmother turns and shows them
her true face, the one that carries a kill –
not a deer, or boar, not a gaur,
no, she's more powerful than that,
walking along the sandy paths
of her natal jungle, so thorns
won't tear the soft pads of her paws.
Only when they point at her strangeness
does she show them how a were-
tigress can drag a leopard in her mouth.

Baghwa

Everyone comes to have their fortunes told
and here comes the village vicar.
But first he must open the gate and pass
between the rockery and rosebed,
        thorn forest and shadow creek.

Oh the cool of the deep-banked stream
where the baghwa lies panting in the dry season.
And when there is water she spreads
her liana-limbs under the ripples
        and there is quiet, such quiet.

My tiger-gran in her garden, clouds scudding
over her face, her flowers all the colours
of childhood – paprika reds, dust yellows,
monsoon blues. And there is the lawn
        beyond the pond – her sacred meadow,

after bamboo and sal tangle with its
langur alarms, chital barks, peacock cries.
There she is in her gypsy finery from jumble sales,
her tarot pack, sitting among savanna stalks
        and lapa grass, wild mint swaying,

her face striped by seedheads,
her ears pinned to every air current.
There she is sniffing the sky, her eyes
closed, nostrils open, every tigress-nerve
        twitching for scent,

her paw with its banyan-work of veins,
the tender pads sheltering vibrations
that rise up the ground to her spine.
What does she see? Does she dare tell Vicar
          how his days are aligned –

which day will be killed, which spared?
Her mouth slightly open, tasting each
bud of his life, a flare of bulbul song.
She rises from her flowery bed and wraps
          the garden around her like a sari,

carries a mountain on her head, back rod-
straight, the rockery sedums trembling,
such is the burden she must bear –
the terror of second sight. Then,
          watch her client walk down the path

from the trek into the core, the tales
he will tell of the séance. How, as she read his palm
her eyes closed to slits and she seemed
to resist the spirits. How they came to her
          easy as a sambar fawn,

how she had to eat them, her powers kept
draining her. How pale she became
then revived after feeding. That moment
she put on her glasses
          at the very end of time

and he saw the sun in the black of her eyes,
while the cards in her hands ran
like deer from the leopard.
The flash of a white-naped woodpecker
          as it crossed his line of sight

and shut its holy fire, here in this Welsh garden
at high summer when the gardener
rested from her labours
and indulged the parishioners.
    It was a sultry afternoon

and yet he'd travelled far, his lifespan
sparkling like a lake, a carcass glinting
on the far bank, fought over by jackals,
a wild boar, vultures that swooped
        to plunge in their beaks.

Baghwa is an Indian tribal name for tiger

Her Washing

I love the boiler and wooden tongs, the mangle
rollers that I turn and turn, to go back
to my Gran's as she takes in neighbours' washing

until everything shines like the giant wood spider webs
I found in Bandhavgarh jungle,
strung between sal and dhok trees,

swaying in the sun like sheets hung to dry,
and her at the centre – the Monday morning of my life.

Landscape with Vultures

The morning was almost over
when I came to Rajbhera Meadow
where hundreds of vultures had gathered.
They held up their wings, fanning the feathers
as if to say aren't we beautiful?
Or drank from the waterhole, or launched themselves
into the air after a run-up like a plane,
to land on a branch just above my head,
silhouetted against the sky like long-necked gods –
griffons from other worlds, death-eaters.
There is so much ugliness on this earth
but they should not be loathed for the way
they plunge their heads into corpses.
I wanted to be brave as them,
to plunge my face in the maggots and gore
and eat until nothing was left
except shining white ribs.
And here they were resting after work, getting on with their lives –
perhaps gossiping, or courting, or just
letting the sun worship each vane of their feathers.
I could see the breeze stir the soft grey down
on their breasts as if it loved them.
The meadow was enchanted
with its hazy backdrop of Bandhavgarh Fort
on its sacred plateau laced with their nests,
and I did not want to leave.
I thought about what happens
after death, how our souls might gather
on some shimmering plain after our descent from the ether,
the whirr of our wings as we perch on the tree of knowledge
staring past humans.

It was as if the carcasses of my life
were purged
just for that half hour
and I was allowed to see a volt of vultures –
some endangered, some rare, for there were Egyptians there,
Kings, Himalayans, and the Indian –
who had all soared in the stratosphere,
birds that can overcome the smell of fear
that must linger on a kill
to be digested by sky-beings.
I wanted to gobble up the poison of the world
and squirt it out in white splatters like summer snow,
then rise
in the alchemical light, clean as the moment of my birth
when the midwife washed my mother's scat from my skin.

Her Half Indian Back

Sit up straight was her mantra,
my Gran of the correct posture
who wore her father's medals, chest out,
as she carried the Legion banner.

Only when I drove through rural India
did I see the women, all rod-backed,
balancing firewood on their heads,
a hay-bale, four bags of cement –

only then did I see her carrying me, not
in her womb, but on her head, held high
over the Channel as she walked
through water to take me to safety.

Flash Forests

Just as an orphaned fawn
will huddle against a wooden deer
used for target practice –

so I cling to you, my grandmother,
while all around us
the forests burn.

~

It is I who turned
the world ash Yggdrasil
to ashes,

I who watched on plasma screens
as koalas charred,
I who saw sloths

with rare eco-systems
on their upside-down fur,
cremated in backdrafts.

~

Let me be your bat pup
and you can be
my ficus religiosa.

I'm hugging what's left –
aerial roots of your hair
I once buried my face in.

I'll roost under
your prayer leaves
until the flames come.

#ExtinctionRebellion

The day will come when papers
will only tell leaf-stories
of blackbirds' quarrels with sparrows.

Their pages will roll back into trees
and the front page will be bark.

Tabloids will be hundred-winged birds
singing earth anthems.

I'll settle into the buttress root of my armchair
and watch ants swarm

to text me secrets from the soil
adding emojis
of all our lost species.

I'll be surrounded by phones
that light up with chlorophyll,
vibrating like workers in their hives –

an apiary of apps.

I'll touch a vanda orchid
and it'll open
easily as hypertext,

everyone will hold leaves
intently as smartphones

to hear them retweet birdsong
from archives.

This is my homepage, where I belong.
This is my wood wide web,

my contour map
with which to navigate
a new internet –

rootlets sparking towards rootlets
underground.

Underground
where resistance is in progress –

fungal friends working in darkness,
their windows blacked out.

Trees of Song

You call us the trees of song
        because when night falls
                we draw the bows of our branches

against our trunks
        and play for our lives.
                When the forest gates open

we let you in,
        start our day's work
                making air, growing wombs

that dream up birds.
        It is we who are singing
                the leopard and langur,

replacing the ones you kill.
        You come dressed as a groom
                all in red

with rifles for branches
        as if you could marry
                your green bride.

We sing the hymns that burn
        at the centre of the earth.
                We call them up

and they surge through us.
        Our bows play so fast
                we self-combust

like brides who don't want to marry,
      who set themselves alight.
            By sunrise all you see

is smoke rising from our stumps
      like morning mist,
            and our spirits are gone.

Her Teeth

Give me my grandmother back, even
the nights when her tiger-teeth shone
in the Steradent glass by her bedside.

Treasure Cupboard

When I die I want to live in your treasure cupboard
behind glass doors, on glass shelves
between the Asian lion and Himalayan wolf.

We'll look out onto your living room,
your floral armchair, the fire where flames
leap like deer over the brass guard.

And in the evening the clothes-horses
will come out dressed in white sheets
so you can wash between them in the tub.

The television will cast black and white stripes
that roar over your face. Nobody
will come to check on you as it monsoons

after the test card has vanished.
When you fall asleep in your chair,
the houseplants will remember their homes

and sing lullabies of jungles
where you lived as a child. Your abandoned
knitting, slumped over the chair arm

like a nesting langur, will always have endless arms.
And for once, I will be the one to tell you
the bedtime story, inventing new details

to keep you spellbound. This time, my dark-skinned
daadi ma, it is the last snow-white tigress
in the wild, who has sapphires for eyes,

who walks into your tent and picks you up
between her fangs and drops you gently
in the crystal cave among her mewling treasures.

A Tailorbird Nest

(for John Keats)

I'm listening

        for the one

who pierces holes

        in two leaves

stitches them

        together

with cobweb

        and plant fibre

Can her green purse

        be our urn?

Perhaps we could chant

        your odes, Keats,

composed not long

        before your death

but still alive

        make ourselves

eggshell light

        speckled with stars

use your music

        to weave

a forest

        from two leaves?

The Anthropocene

A bride wears a train
        of three thousand
                peacock plumes

She walks down the aisle
        like a planet
                trailing her seas

every wave an eye
        shivering with the memory
                of the display

how the trees turned
        to watch as the bird
                raised the fan of his tail –

emerald forests
        bronze atolls
                lapis islands

every eye
        a storm
                held in abeyance

Snow Leopardskin Jacket

On my thirteenth birthday I've saved up
enough pocket money to buy a leopardskin jacket
and prowl the streets like a new queen.
But when my mother comes for Christmas
she slaps me, says fur is for the hunting set,
and since mine is 'faux', I look like a whore.

I know what that word means, and under
rosettes I've been wearing like medals
for reaching puberty, under rose stains
like a first period, my skin has blanched.
Her slap wipes away the taste of my first date,
the kiss from the farmer's son.

> *I am the juvenile cub sent to the mountain.*
> *I am the last snow ghost on earth.*
> *I draw on the walls of my cave*
> *to remember my teenage, scratch them*
> *on the rock face – all the animals I've lost.*

> *I ate blue sheep raw in the red sheets,*
> *lonely as the world's last ice-cat.*
> *My snowy wastes, my hunger.*
> *The moon kissed stigmata on my fur –*
> *the stars left love bites over my body.*

Grandala

You tell me there are birds so blue
they seem to be painting the sky.
They surge like a flock of waves,

an ocean that's forgotten its weight,
that lands on pines, making them
burst into heavenly fruit.

Or maybe we are just the palette God
mixes His colours upon, you say,
and He is repainting the planet

as it breaks. You lean in close
and whisper, *Don't let anyone tell you*
the world is ugly, I have seen

a grandala open its beak and
show me the gold leaf inside.
I remember this when I need you. I think

of the jewellery box of your mouth
where the colours are hatching.
Or maybe God is painting

creatures for us from His mirror –
birds celestial as Himalayas
that launch from glass cliffs

to crash through our atmosphere.
What does God feed them in His aviary
with its cages of space-time?

I think whatever He might be,
He made you, my grandmother – no one
knows the story of your origins,

for all I know you were raised by tigers.
All you had to go on was your father
warning you to beware his wife. *Don't*

let anyone tell you the world is ugly,
he whispered. *Better you find yourself*
a tigress for a mother than stay with her

once I am gone. It was that day the grandala
appeared, you say, *they wheeled*
above our house and landed on snow.

We'd travelled as far as the Annapurnas.
Daddy wanted to show me earth's roof
and one landed on a bush beside me,

opened its beak like a music box
containing the sun. Maybe we are just
splinters of the shattered world

God is trying to fit back, I say.
Or it's the birds that are painting
themselves into lazuli icons,

their chicks fledging in my optic nerves.
Maybe it is always the first morning of summer
and I'm opening the wings of my eyes.

Jungle Owlet

What you didn't tell me
is how poachers cut off their claws

and break bones in one wing
so they can't perch or fly,

that their eyes are sold as pujas,
boiled in broth, so herdsmen

can see in the dark.
You didn't say how sorcerers

keep their skulls, their barred feathers,
their livers and hearts,

or how they drink their blood and tears.
You didn't mention how a tortured

owl will speak like a young girl
to reveal where treasure is buried.

My kind granny who took me in
when I was homeless,

who sat down this very evening
after I had gone to bed

and wrote Mother a stern letter,
telling her that she must take me back,

it doesn't matter where – Paris, Wales,
Timbuktu. No more excuses,

you are tired. And here, your slanted writing
is almost illegible, but what

I think it says is that you cannot
look after a teenage owlet.

You use your favourite pet name.
I've never spoken of this before.

I call it up my gullet from the pit
at the bottom of my thirteenth year,

along with my crushed bones,
my stolen blood, and I spit it out

through my torn-off beak, in
language that passes for human.

Her Glasses

My grandmother's glasses are a greenhouse
behind which luxurious flowers grow,
species I will never name, or find again.

Her last glance back at her childhood jungle
trembles there, watered by monsoons
but I have never seen her cry. She closed

the glass doors as I said goodbye. She
waved at me as the taxi drove me away –
her blinds came down against my fierce rays.

My Velvet

The first thing that happened when we arrived
at the new house, the last act
of my teens – let me remember it, even
the pain, even the sawing sound
as I sat obedient on the wooden chair.
Let me commemorate my antlers, how
I used to admire each new tine in the mirror,
above my doe eyes that boys liked.
Let me have one glance at the human
who stands above me with her hacksaw,
who says they must be short now – stubs
of my pretty velvets. I do not flinch,
even though blood pours down my cheeks.
Mother says they are made of keratin
and don't hurt, but they were pulsing
with nerves, enough for me to avoid
low branches. I have left the wild
and my herd. I am a tame fawn now,
childish, so that Mother feels better.
She scrubs my face clean of shadow
and eyeliner. She sucks the blood
from the antlers to make herself young.

Clouded Girl

(after Marie Howe)

If I could have been a creature,
maybe a clouded leopard,

eyes brimming with homesickness
for far flung star-clouds,

fangs in my mouth
like lunar sabres from another era –

but I padded in slippers
so quiet

even the air didn't hear me
climb the tree of my mind.

And if I went to my child self now
to comfort her,

she'd stare past me
and still see her mother

wide as the enveloping globe
she had to claw her way out of,

the child's glance grazing
the rim of our atmosphere

before her leap to extinction.

My Grecian Urn

When I read your poem, I'm fourteen again,
   searching for a way back to you, Keats.
It's dark inside but my pencil passes
   through the stems of your lines
on the trail of a tigress
   whose black flames are dryads.
     This is how I slip into plant time,
   become your foster-child.
How many years can I hide here –
     crayons filling the paper with leaves,

inkpots casting kaleidoscopes of trees?
   Only you, Keats, know that the eyes
I'm drawing belong to a tigress
   who leads us to a ravine
where cubs lie panting in a cave.
   I'm on the brink, peering down
     into the altar of my life.
Who are these coming to the sacrifice?
   Who brings the heifer lowing at the skies?
   Who dressed her with garlands?

Monkeys bark a warning
   from the trunk of a mahua tree
but we peer down, drunk on nectar,
   into the pit where Bhitri lives –
even her name means 'innermost forest'.
   How many corpses litter her porch?
     I've been drawing them all my life,
lying in my room, quiet as ash
   while my mother calls –
     If I concentrate, I don't hear her.

The tigress drags the calf down
    to her cubs. She pauses, silhouetted
against sunset, the heifer almost
    full grown – a house pet with
bridal frangipani around her neck,
    her eyes open. She has just stopped
        breathing. My red crayon listens.
If I hold my breath I can hear, down
    in the gorge, what I cannot see –
        teeth crunching bones, tearing flesh.

Every time it's a miracle, what comes out
    of this urn. I draw until all my crayons
are used. With the last stub of green, you vanish,
    Keats, and I'm back in my room,
still fourteen. Obediently, I climb downstairs
    to face my mother. She stands there
        wearing a bridal wreath around her neck.
I sit at the table with her, meek as a tiger
    who's been declawed, defanged,
        who can't remember the jungle where she reigned.

Indian Paradise Flycatcher

your tail two comets
    of ice crystals
        your face a night-
           blue sheen

           as if dipped
    in starlight
your wings snowdrifts
from a past climate

you descend
    in a heat haze
        and when you dip
           into a pool

           you're a pen
    sky-writing
on a mirror
a flick of flakes

melting
    a jet's contrails
        telling us
           about a sun fuelled

        by frost
    Too fast for my eye
your tail streamers
weave an alphabet

to cool the earth
        you dinosaur-relic
                little white flag
                        from the Holocene

Wild Dogs

You didn't tell me about wild dogs – Phantom,
Hellhound, Jungle Devil, Kali's Bitch –
they come with their convex muzzles,
russet fur, scissoring teeth. Almost from extinction
they appear, whistling to one another,
and the king of the forest is afraid.
He must stand his ground, not run, for then
they will hurl themselves at his bowels
and draw out the long intestines, start eating them
while he's fleeing. One swipe of his paw
cracks a spine and five are down, but the rest
continue, biting his nose, gouging an eye.
Yet more make for his thighs to tear off the balls.
They keep close to his belly, behind
the great claws, under slashing fangs,
where they get to work ripping his chest
until the ribs are exposed. And now I know why
you didn't tell me about Indian dholes.
What drives the ravenous female to eat the beating
heart of the jungle? O god of tigers, O tiger-star
roaring in your bleeding sky – tell me, does it take
a pack of wild dogs to brave your fire?
Who made the demons? What constellation forged their atoms?
What chance do I have when they come for me,
gnawing my body's tender parts while I'm still alive?

The Tiger Game

When I went to live with my mother
she'd play the Tiger Game.
I was always the Tiger, blinds down,
lights off, all furniture removed.

She'd sit in the centre of the room
with a revolver. I'd take off my shoes,
empty my pockets, and glide.
She only aimed at my legs

if she heard a sound. I learnt
the silence of stalking,
became mute, invisible,
my body was a blackout.

I hid in my room doing homework
all night – every day was a night.
By 'room' I mean my head.
In my head a jungle grew

and in that jungle I escaped.
Once, I stumbled against the wall
and Maman fired, hitting my chest.
But it was my fault for falling, I

caused her to break the rules, aim
higher than allowed. Even though
her gun was made up, the sounds
she did with her mouth could kill.

Nilgai

Bihar, 1st September 2019

This antelope shot
but still alive

this 'vermin'
shoved in the deep pit

by the earthmover
mud tipped over him

until all that remains
before his head vanishes

are his eyes
staring at us

like the twin barrels
of a shotgun

Prize Photograph

And this wild elephant, crossing State Highway 9 –
his footprints lakes for dragonflies and bees –

does not yet know the chaff of a howdah,
ankle chains, or the sting of the bull hook.

His mother is ahead, her ears flapping
for his rumbles that she also feels through her feet.

Only now her feet are burning, and she's
closed her ears to the firecrackers, the jeers

of the mob protecting their fields. Already
one farmer has hung himself when his crop

and home were trampled – how could he feed his family?
And one woman has been crushed to death.

The men lob tar firebombs at the invaders –
go back jungli haathi! they shout, banging

on tin drums. The matriarch runs from the noise,
doesn't hear her calf scream, his back legs alight.

Hell is now and here the caption will say
as Biplap Hazra clicks the shot of his life.

Hatha Jodi

There is a language to describe
what I saw next
but no one speaks it

It has a body this language
it hisses and bites
has a split lizard tongue

a split lizard penis

this organ laid on the table
in a secret backroom
next to many of its kind

First you have to enter the jewelled forest
and track the scaled one
they call monitor

then you tie his legs together
wrap his long tail round his neck

Next you make a fire
wait until it crackles
and you hold your prize
alive over the flames

burning his genitals
until the shy forked hemipenis comes out

and then you cut it off
at the root
where the two members meet

the root where two hands
seem to be praying

Hatha jodi you say – *praying hands*

sacred herb that grows
only in Nepal and Madhya Pradesh
will bring you luck

This language is sold
all over the internet
to buyers in America – England even

Tell me – what language does the lizard speak
and who hears it?

Spotted Deer

To be spotlit
like a doe
in the forest
at dawn

I would risk
all the leopards
and tigers
even my father's gun

To be spotlit
like a bride
on the aisle
of this cathedral

I would wear
a deer dress
of stars, my legs
light as sunrays

Isn't death sparks
of holy fire?
Better to have heard
the leaves praying

once as the sun
was rising
than remained
safe in the dark

Pangolin

Tell me, you who do not believe –
who are these humans in the restaurant,

these Homo Sapiens, half a million years young,
while a pangolin, who is eighty million

years older, floats in a jar of rice wine.
How did she get there? And this one

the waiter brings to the table alive
to have her throat slit, her blood poured

into their wine as aphrodisiac.
Tell me, wise ones who do not believe

in surgeons who operate without anaesthetic –
why is this freezer in the kitchen

crammed with armour-plated survivors?
Why are two-tonne sacks of their scales

overflowing onto the floor, countless floors?
Witness how this humble pangolin clings

to the hollow of a tree, while hunters
tug her tail. Watch them light a fire

to smoke her out, then take her to their hut
and calm her with a machete, many cuts

until she is almost dead but not enough,
because there is a cauldron of water

she must now endure, held by her head
so her tail boils first.

Why, you might ask, does anyone do this
and the answer could be money –

they have debts, medical bills, and one
pangolin is like winning the lottery,

you could say her scales are coins
of a rare vintage, her pelt forged

by the great goldsmith in the sky,
her meat a rare delicacy for the rich.

One pangolin, perhaps the last.
Tell me, you who do not believe in Aryans

who once pronounced themselves
the master race, and thought others to be subhuman,

what is the mastery that makes us
drive other races, other species, to extinction?

Swamp Deer

The barasingha bears his twenty-tined rack
like a crucified forest

he alone must carry
on the Golgotha of his brow,

head-wood he has decorated
with hyacinths and watergrass,

a great egret riding on the crown
like a holy ghost.

The buck swims in the flood
bearing his axletree of antlers,

he crosses the highway
with all the birds of Kaziranga

balanced on each fork,
and in every beak a living leaf

held out to us like the host.

Barasingha

(for Jangarh Singh Shyam)

I was nineteen when I came face-to-face with the swamp deer.
He came out of the fog, his black eyes full of dawn.

On his head he bore my forest – teak and evergreen sal
that trailed reeds from the marsh. His fur was sunlit earth.

The Narmada River thundered from his antlers,
turmeric huts of my village draped around twelve tines –

I could hear my mother laugh as she washed on the bank.
From the spotted parsa jhad flower I learnt to make dots dance –

the first time I dipped my brush in bright poster colours
tremors went through my body. I painted the barasingha's blue aura,

his ears ringing with shrieks of jungle babblers.
He towers above me, even in this strange country

where I have not slept for weeks. All I hear are his quavering calls.
I draw chevrons, thickets of zigzags, meadows

of windblown stripes, constellations of leaves, and always
I hum the old songs, so he will carry me back to the forest.

In the hungry hours the rain on my skylight is his hooves
pacing the heavens, his horns lit up with strobe lightning

like the city at night. It is he who lowers a noose
from the ceiling fan and tells me the gods are angry

that I have shown their likeness. I will float onto my mount
the way the brush glides on the paper, in a leap

of everlasting joy. When I arrive in his pasture
he will shake his neck as if shrugging off a shower,

let the motion ripple down his spine – and I will be
the spray rising from his back in a halo of drops.

Brown Fish Owl

1

Once, I lived in a mango tree above
shallows where I waded for fish.

I have hunted pond herons, a monitor lizard,
and eaten putrid crocodile.

I have survived five million years.
It is said my feathers sing when I fly.
It is said my calls are almost human,

but my eyes burn like twin suns
in this night that tastes of dirt.

I'm calling now, *tu-whoo-tu* –
who keeps me outside their door?

Tu-whoo-hu? But they don't answer
so I call again – *boom-o-boom* –

I think they must hear because
my voice is almost human

even muffled by a foot of soil.
Tu-whoo-hu has buried me alive?

2

I was inside and needed air, heard
a brown fish owl calling.

The voice was muffled like someone buried.
I went back in and told my host,

who said, *that's my lucky charm*
which means I'll win this election.

Ever since, I have heard the owl in my mirror,
I have seen two gold eyes peer through silver
as if fishing in the shallows

and thought how priceless eyes are –
coins that blind if looked at directly,

money that must be buried under soul soil,
star dirt. Feathers ray around them –
brown wings that sing as they fly.

Tiger Myth

They said to me – don't write about
        the tiger-shaped universe,

only its stripes spiralling about you
        in weather fronts and galaxies.

They said – don't meet its gaze,
        its eyes are dying stars.

They told me instead to go to a clearing
        in the Milky Forest

where a tiger lies skinned.
        Describe that, they said.

And my words were its stripes
        cutting across the page,

the ripple of its ringed tail
        one of creation's cobras –

an endless vowel speeding
        towards extinction.

And I saw that sentences could be fur
        stripped from the living power,

that they were cooling
        as I tried to write them.

There was no roar, just a whimper,
        which told me it was still alive.

Then they asked – who
        is the hunter, who the hunted?

while elephants of gravity
        lumbered all around us.

My father's rifle leant against the wall
        like a tired flamingo

as the voices murmured, and a bee
        hummed like a bullet.

Noor

How often have I taken this path that leads
to a sambar doe? The one where the tigress

grabs my hind paw and won't let go.
Noor pouncing on me as I buckle under her weight.

Noor with her fangs around my windpipe.
Noor, sun queen of Ranthambore.

Her coat is the beaded bamboo forest.
Her face above mine is my star-face, the one

I always wanted, always knew I was a doe-tigress
with my veins dripping from my mouth,

Noor ripping my belly open, with its sweet
grasses and herbs. Noor on me like the stag.

My belly heaving like when the fawn first appears
and I lick the blood and eat my placenta, and

when the fawn nuzzles my teats it is a tiger
feeding on my intestines while I am still alive.

Common Map

(Cyrestis thyodamas)

What are a map's antennae?
What is a map's abdomen?
What happens when maps mate –
do they lay new lands?

My grandmother cups the mapwing
in her hands, she is still a child
when she shows me her empty palms –
the occupant long migrated.

My country was free as childhood
she says, *but I can still feel it*
beat against my skin –
heavy as Himalayas.

Here – you hold it for a while.

Sometimes, when I press her butterfly
against the mirror, contour lines appear,
translucent wings
of the lightest mountain.

Passport

I sew leaves together for the passport,
a slug trails the finest mirror-writing.

And the watermark? Printed by an ocean.

At the border an owl stamps
my passport with his claw.

Only he can see the pages fall
every winter, regrow each spring.

My passport is round
but there are those
who still believe it's flat,

that an ant will sail off the edge
into the vacuum of an airport terminal.

My biometric fingerprints
have a scent only a jackal can read.

A woodpecker types me
a residence permit
from his high office,

but still no word from the government.
Will they send me that verdict –
prepare to leave our kingdom!

Home Office –
I am a citizen of the wild,
my address is a cloud,

my date of birth
the innermost ring of earth's crust.

And the country of my birth?

Have you heard the chants
of the snowy tree crickets?

One enters my room like a violinist
from a far galaxy,
who knows how to sing
the word 'foreigner' in my language

until the whole house
trills with his kyrie eleison –

Lord, have mercy on strangers.

The Superb Lyrebird

mimics a kookaburra, dingo bark,
      growls of koalas.

Ground dweller, poor flier,
      flees on foot or freezes

when faced with threat.
      To make his lek he clears

bushland of brush
      that sparks wildfires –

nature's forester.
      He flips his tail plumes

over his head – two lyrates
      and a smoky fan of quills

that he shakes in sync
      with his song – a medley

of camera shutters, crying babes,
      car alarms, rifle shots,

repeats them
      between bursts of rainbow finch,

cockatoo, galah. Then
      trees creaking in wind,

gusts through their crowns.
      When the flames come

he fast-forwards a repertoire
     of all the songbirds

his ancestors learnt –
     fairy wren, jewel-babbler.

Even now, he's dancing
     to new sounds –

water-plane crash, firestorm surge,
     his superb lyre alight.

Her Bedroom

How often have I dreamt of this room
with its sunlit branches, its oxygen –
plants overwintering all around us?
We are fruit bats roosting under leaves,
chattering when we should be asleep.
I am two months old, a clinging bat pup
in my upside-down world.
It is always daytime, even at night,
dream-sun pouring through skylights.
Each mama is over a hundred, the age
you would be now, my grandmother –
let me snuggle under your wings.
The leaves around your silver hair
are ivory ghosts, every capillary shining.
If I could, I would wrap your body
in a cloth, place a dummy in your mouth
and set you down in the cot
like a rescued flying fox.
Your hands hook mine, scorched,
as if you've been hurtling through time tunnels.
It's my turn to brush your russet fur,
clean your nose with cotton buds, mend
those huge ears that have been listening
to star sonar. Your black eyes
are open wide in astonishment
at finding yourself through the mirror,
roles reversed. Look at how
I've prepared this room for your recovery.

Night Garden

When they took me away from you, I waited,
your hair moonlight,

the blue rinses like blossoms
that drifted through my Paris window.

I lay on the camp bed, an infant longing
for you to say goodnight, to tell me

once again the story of the leopard tree
where you hid all evening, the acacia thorns

that scratched like claws.
So I called you down, my leopard-gran.

And when the moon was full, I let its blessing
slip through my pores, to root in my body,

knew you were at work in the star-soil
and would send me the ghost of your garden.

Just before dawn, a breeze floated through
the broken pane, like the last wisp of your breath.

I saw the black flowers of night open
and scatter pollen like Hindi vowels –

as if you were once again talking in your sleep
in what I thought was moon-language

or what a lotus might say if it could speak
with its feral mouth.

Forest Guard

I want the world's presidents to live here
alone,
        one after the other,
                in my shack, with no gun –

just walls that let in moonlight and owlsong.

Little pay, but one twenty-four carat pugmark
is priceless.

I want the fool who calls the Amazon rainforest
a wasteland

and he who would turn my reserve
into a golf course

to lie on my bed, while sunlight
pierces slats of the walls
to cast stripes on his skin.

Let them be pretenders of power!

      ~

This is my second life.
The empress ended my first.

I was in a paddy field, luring her
away from the village
back to safety
        and she swiped my face.

I was out for three months.

I'm telling you this because
with my second life
I returned to the forest to guard her.

~

Here is my beat map, my night shift.
Here is my path to the hide,
my notebook to record every scat and spoor.

The stars wait in their auditorium,
Orion is abroad, that smuggler of sky animals.

Here she comes in her coat of gasoline.

Here is the mob that set my empress alight.
I also was dowsed, skull split by an axe.

Here come her cubs in their seraphim coats.
Over charred stumps
they scent-mark, they spray,

they rub their faces against bark.

Jungle Cat

When a cat walks through the sliding doors
at first you think it's just a stray, then see
the pointed ears with tufts, ringed tail
and legs, and realise it's a jungle cat.
You daren't blink, breathe even, the air
holds your last breath and draws it out
while you look and look at the speckled tan coat,
the yellow eyes that have not noticed you yet.
You sometimes wish you'd stayed like that
with the brief visitor, Tala Zone
spread before you through the patio doors
and the perimeter fence, beyond which
the glamour of life unfolds at dream pitch.
You sometimes forget to breathe just
remembering it, her sniffing the doorframe
just as you work out what she is, and
maybe this is her tenth life, maybe she's
unravelled the mummy bandages of the afterlife
and you are glimpsing yours,
lying on this bed while she wanders in
bringing the gift of just what it's like
to really feel alive, to have every hair
on your body rise to become taut,
every nerve alert and quivering.
So now, when your image comes to me
I see your quiet face that welcomed
the wild one of our world, her portrait
juxtaposed on yours, every precious inch
mirroring the inner core of the forest.

Mahaman's Face through Binoculars

The meadow grasses are feather strokes,
          greens drift like smoke from a censer.

Here is the ghost of a stripe –
          the fur-edge of a lightning flash.

Then, the raising of the triple discs
          that frame her face like a trinity,

the black birdwing arabesques
          above her brows are holy ghosts.

The pure white chin is creation's brush
          loaded with mist at the beginning of time.

Her jaws ajar, a gate of horn
          I must pass through.

In her left eye, a blue dot sparkles –
          reflection of sky between blades

of lemongrass and vetivers,
          as if Earth is rising in her iris.

For a Coming Extinction

(after W.S. Merwin)

You whom we have named Charger, Challenger,
Great King, and Noor the shining one,

now that you are at the brink of extinction,
I am writing to those of you

who have reached the black groves of the sky,
where you glide beneath branches of galaxies,

your fur damasked with constellations,
tell him who sits at the centre of the mystery,

that we did all we could.
That we kept some of you alive

in the prisons we built for you.
You tigers of Amur and Sumatra,

of Turkey and Iran, Java and Borneo,
and you – Royal Bengals, who lingered last.

Tell the one who would judge
that we are innocent of your slaughter.

That we kiss each pugmark,
the water trembling inside

as if you had just passed.
Masters of ambush and camouflage,

hiding behind astral trees,
invisible as always,

when we gaze up at the night,
when we look lightyears into the past –

we see your eyes staring down at us.

Her Staircase

(after Do Ho Suh's 'Staircase III')

There is a staircase of red gauze
floating just below the high ceiling,
steps she could never ascend
                            in bone and flesh

but here she lies under the flight,
as she rises from her broken body,
the neck that cracked on impact with concrete,

            here she is somersaulting once
                            up the ether-blood stairs

where stars are the trains of white peacocks
passing through red shift,

all the shades of celeste to royal, core
of suns, violent fabrics

of the spirit world.

Upside-down stairway, your material
hovers like a space ship

for she thinks she is at the top,
                    might still be sleeping there,

will unfold her head from under her chest
and soar,
            blood returning into her mouth
                        from the coconut welcome mat,
                        and into her heart, where it pumps.

Her life floats through her, step
by step, and she is getting smaller, lighter,
as if her bones are made of air,

until she arrives on the landing, foot
poised.
       Winglets play around her ankle,
her hand on the banister,
                  now whipped
back
       to straighten her nightie

as she walks backwards through the door
and into bed, where she falls asleep

       while below her the red staircase
       sways softly in a breeze

because someone has finally opened
the front door
           and discovered her.

Kew Gardens

You're even smaller than the last time I took you
and we are dizzy from climbing the spiral staircase,
its double helix to the canopy walkway,
eye to eye with royal palms and giant bamboo,
inside the palm house near the end of your life.
We reel, peering down through leaves
to the realm of flowers extinct in the wild.
Kew, Kew, how we love the perfumes
that we inhale like addicts, the safe air,
the glass hull like an upturned ark.
We haven't yet been to the vanda orchids.
We are still making our way, delayed
once again by filmy ferns. Oh, the filmy ferns
where your face shines green.
I'm almost back inside the central dome
and you're alive again under a haze of mist
as the humidifier switches on with a metered hiss.
We're listening to the recorded rainforest birds
and I'm carrying your walking stick,
while you stroke treeferns, Jurassic cycads
with your rheumatic hand – knotted and veined rosary
I fumble for, reciting the five joyful,
five luminous, five sorrowful and five
glorious mysteries, of the one who saved me
and saves me every day, while we make
our pilgrimage to the world's oldest pot plant.

Her Flowers

Just before she died, my grandmother glanced
out of her bedroom window and saw her garden

bloom one last time – with white chrysanthemums,
lavender peonies, prize dahlias,

cascades of red-hot pokers, delphinium sparks.
Did the fireworks wake her?

Muzzy from sleeping pills, my grandmother
got out of bed and started to go downstairs,

missed her step and thrust out her hand to save herself,
but the clothes drying on the banister

gave way, and down she hurtled
breaking her neck, while bouquets of lupins

exploded into the early hours.
Each November 5th I think of the passing of one

who seemed like a goddess to me, her sky-high flowers
when I stood in the heaven of her garden –

the mountains of her rockery, the shrubbery,
savanna of her lawn and the honeysuckles

with their anthers of fire, their buds opening
with a thunder-crack, the fuse wire of their stems.

Sky Ladder

(after Cai Guo-Qiang)

Quick, before the sun
rises, get up one more
time, my grandmother.
The artist won't mind
if you borrow
his sky ladder.
Place your foot
on the bottom rung
and keep climbing,
even though
you're a skeleton
with a broken neck
from falling downstairs
on Guy Fawkes night.
The ladder is wrapped
in gunpowder, and he's
lit the touchpaper.
Your bones are ascending
firecrackers.
You're half a kilometre
high now, halfway
to the universe,
my joy-gardener.
I hope you find a
garden with rich black
soil for your black
roses, hybrids like you –
half white half Indian,
half woman half flower,
their roots twined
through your skull,

you who were transplanted
among the pale roses
of a British family.
Your skin now a mix
of photons and soot.
What do you find up there?
Is there a hothouse?
Are there alien hands
with deft brushes
pollinating stars?
Remember how
your tomatoes kept
yielding more planets?
Are there constellations
of exotic fruit now
you've reached the top?
Have you gone back
enough in space-time
to when you were alive?
The ladder is charred,
the hot air balloon
that held it up
is about to collapse.
The explosions are over.
Cai showers his head
with champagne, as his
100-year-old granny
watches on her cell phone.
Did you see it? He asks,
did you hear the whoosh,
the rat–tat–tat
at the starry door?
You can go back
to sleep now, he tells her.
Go back to sleep,

I tell you, but first,
if you're hungry,
have a snack on one
of those quasars,
before you dream again
of the tumble
through air to
the stone landing,
fireworks the last
thing you hear.

Walking Fire

It's high summer and the grass hisses where the tigress treads,
her pads soundless on the tinder track.
Her flanks sway, the cubs cool in their amniotic sacs.

She is a walking fire
                    her glance a flare
                    that singes my lashes.

I seem to be watching her through a veil of snow or ash –
the sky as I know it falling   falling

and when her face comes into focus
it's like the membrane between us tears.

She brushes against the jeep as she saunters past
on the long patrol of her realm,
                    her fur dripping after a soak in the stream.

                    Can you see me, Gran? I ask, *I'm as close*
                    to a tiger as you once were, but I won't touch.
                    A baby wouldn't alarm her, but I would.

You're sitting opposite, saying, *It was like staring at a frozen sun.*

Your eyes grow coal-black
as you think of the day you were left alone in a tent.

I'm staring at the fire in your living room, anthracite
glowing with forests of our Coal Age,
                    flickers of fern   horsetail   clubmoss

embers spitting onto the mat
                    like sabre tooths springing from a cave –

that split second when we startle
and everyone is still alive
                              even my first cat
not yet given stripes by the combine harvester
as he lay curled in corn.

I'd walk over hot coals to get back to you, just to ask
one more question about your tiger.

But you were only a baby
and probably you only remembered remembering
not the thing itself.
                        Just as now, I'm only half-
remembering the ghost of your fire
where we sit like two Ice Age queens
worshipping the heat

while underneath us the compressed beds of trees
            buckle under mountain-building.

The tigress has passed by now, and is ahead on the path,
rolling over the sand, belly-up, revelling in her power.

Already she's spawned three sets of cubs
and they've forged their own empires.

When she leaps onto a stag
                        the whole world slows
to hear the grass speak from inside the deer.

                              Slows enough
to listen to what trees have to say
with the mouths of storms through their leaves.

When I've firewalked through the dawn of your death
my feet scorched
                    on the cinder path to your house,
when I've opened the gate of your garden –

            like opening the gate to Tala Zone
            where wildlife is almost safe –

I will land in your armchair in the deepest cave.

And then   Gran   we will talk again
about the forests that once reigned on earth

the mysteries of beasts who passed through them,
the flames of their spirits surging under fur,
not one spark escaping.

How even their roars
are relics of when the great woods blazed.
                    How it was we
who discovered fire and with our knowledge

lit the fuse.

ACKNOWLEDGEMENTS

My thanks to the editors of the following publications, where some of these poems were first published, sometimes in other versions: *Ambit, bath magg, Brixton Review of Books, For the Silent* (Indigo Dreams), *Island* (Tasmania), *Manhattan Review, Mslexia, New Humanist, New Statesman, One Hand Clapping, Poetry* (USA), *Poetry London, The Poetry Review, Royal Academy of Arts Magazine, The Rialto, Shi Lin* (China), *Stand: The Ecopoetics Issue, Wasafiri,* and *Wild Court.*

I am enormously grateful to the Royal Literary Fund for generous financial assistance while I was working on this book. I am grateful to the Royal Society of Literature for a Literature Matters Award in 2018, which allowed me time to write the first half of *Tiger Girl.* My deepest thanks to them and the judges for the RSL Ondaatje Prize 2018 for *Mama Amazonica,* as it enabled me to travel to India to observe wild tigers and other fauna and flora. I am also grateful to the Society of Authors for an Authors' Foundation grant in 2019, which allowed me to return to Bandhavgargh Tiger Reserve in Madhya Pradesh, and also to have time to write the second half of the book. Warm thanks to naturalist Saily Gokhale, my main guide in the Kanha and Bandhavgarh forests, who managed to book the premium Tala core zone at Bandhavgarh for my second trip, and to Ajju the Gypsy jeep driver on countless safaris; thanks to him I was once within touching range of Spot-T, the queen tigress of Tala Zone.

Thanks to the editors of *Royal Academy of Arts Magazine,* who commissioned 'Surprised!'. The poem responds to Henri Rousseau's painting 'Surprised! (Tiger in a Tropical Storm)'. Thanks also to the Keats-Shelley Memorial Association, who commissioned 'A Tailorbird Nest' for their book *Odes for John Keats.* The first few stanzas of '#ExtinctionRebellion' started life in my poem 'The Spring', commissioned by the Royal Society of Literature for their *Peace Poetry* anthology.

A poem from this book, 'Indian Paradise Flycatcher', won the 2020 Keats-Shelley Poetry Prize. My thanks to the judges and organisers.

'Her Flowers' was inspired by a firework event 'Ethereal Flowers' by Chinese artist Cai Guo-Qiang. 'Sky Ladder' was inspired by the video made of his successful firework installation in the 'Sky Ladder' series, realised at Huiyu Island Harbour, Quanzhou, Fujian. Lines in my poem draw on interviews with Cai about the process and event. 'Her Staircase' was inspired by the Korean artist Do Ho Suh's 'Staircase III', installed at Tate Modern in 2011. 'Barasingha' is dedicated to the memory of the Pardhan Gond painter Jangarh Singh Shyam (1962–2001), whose painting 'The story of the tiger and the boar' graces my cover. The barasingha motif was central to his practice. I am indebted to Biplap Hazra for his photograph which provoked my poem 'Prize Photograph' and to John Vaillant's account of the Tiger Hunting game, in his book *The Tiger*, which I drew on for my poem 'The Tiger Game'.

Thank you to the sisterhood that is Iphigenia for their support. Thank you to everyone at Bloodaxe Books, especially to my editor Neil Astley for his dedication, encouragement and editing. Finally, thank you, as always, to Brian Fraser for his patient, invaluable comments on the poems.